CORE LANGUAGE SKILLS

Abbreviations

Kara Murray

PowerKiDS press.

New York

Published in 2015 by The Rosen Publishing Group, Inc.
29 East 21st Street, New York, NY 10010

First Edition

Editor: Sarah Machajewski
Book Design: Reann Nye

Photo Credits: Cover Steve Debenport/E+/Getty Images; p. 5 Carol Yepes/Moment Open/Getty Images; p. 7 michaeljung/Shutterstock.com; p. 9 2xSamara.com/Shutterstock.com; p. 13 bahareh khalili naftchali/Shutterstock.com; p. 14 Tetra Images/Getty Images; p. 15 dhorsey/Shutterstock.com; p. 16 http://en.wikipedia.org/wiki/Federal_Bureau_of_Investigation#mediaviewer/File:FBI_Evidence_Response_Team.jpg; p. 17 SuperStock/SuperStock/Getty Images; p. 19 violetblue/Shutterstock.com; p. 21 Compassionate Eye Foundation/Robert Daly/OJO Images/Iconica/Getty Images.

Library of Congress Cataloging-in-Publication Data

Murray, Kara.
Abbreviations / by Kara Murray.
p. cm. — (Core language skills)
Includes index.
ISBN 978-1-4777-7365-9 (pbk.)
ISBN 978-1-4777-7366-6 (6-pack)
ISBN 978-1-4777-7364-2 (library binding)
1. Abbreviations, English. 2. Acronyms. 3. English language — Juvenile literature. I. Murray, Kara. II. Title.
PE1693.M87 2015
423.1—d23

Manufactured in the United States of America

CPSIA Compliance Information: Batch #CW15PK: For Further Information contact Rosen Publishing, New York, New York at 1-800-237-9932

CONTENTS

WHAT DOES THAT STAND FOR?

Have you ever come across a group of letters that doesn't look like a word? Maybe all the letters are **capitalized**, or maybe it's very short with a period after it. This is called an abbreviation (uh-bree-vee-AY-shun). An abbreviation is a shortened form of a word, phrase, or name. It's formed by using letters from the word or phrase that's being shortened.

We use abbreviations to save time when we're writing. Abbreviations also take up less space on a page. We use abbreviations so often you've probably seen them before. Let's learn how to make and use them!

Figure It Out

Why do we use abbreviations?

Find the answer to this question and the others in this book on page 22.

We use abbreviations in all kinds of writing. They're very helpful when we send letters through the mail!

Mr. David Jones Sr.
35 Elm St.
Any Town, NY 00000

Mrs. Green
123 Main St.
Apt. 203
Any Town, NY 00000

SHORTENED TITLES

We often use abbreviations when we use a title. A title comes before or after somebody's name. It tells you something about a person. It may tell you if they're a man or woman, if they're married, or how much schooling they've had. Using titles shows respect for someone.

Titles are almost always abbreviated. "Mr." is an abbreviation for "mister," a man. "Mrs." is an abbreviation for a word that means "married woman." "Dr." is an abbreviation for "doctor," which is a title that **describes** the level of education someone has. Title abbreviations are always capitalized and end with a period.

Figure It Out

The following names have titles that are abbreviated. What do they tell you about the person?

Mrs. Taylor
Mr. Gupta
Dr. Brown
John David Sr.

Dr. Brown   Mr. Gupta   Mrs. Taylor

If a father and son have the same name, titles can tell you who's the dad and who's the child. "Sr." is the abbreviation for "senior," or the dad. "Jr." is the abbreviation for "junior," or the child.

TELLING TIME

You may know something happens at 6 o'clock, but there are two 6 o'clocks in a day. How do you know if it's in the morning or evening? We use the abbreviations "a.m." and "p.m." to help us. The abbreviation "a.m." is used for morning. It means "before noon." The abbreviation "p.m." means "after noon." These abbreviations are very important. They keep us on time!

Imagine you're having a birthday party. You want your friends to come over after dinner at 7 o'clock. Make sure to write "p.m." on the **invitation**, or they may come over before breakfast!

Figure It Out

Many school days begin at 8:00. Which abbreviation should you use for this time, "a.m." or "p.m."?

YOU'RE INVITED!

What: ___My Birthday Party!___

Where: ___My House___

When: ___7:00 p.m.___

Abbreviations for time let us know when things happen.
That way, we won't ever miss school, parties, or TV shows!

9

TACKLING THE CALENDAR

Every month of the year and day of the week has a name. Some of the names are long. Abbreviations help us save time and space when we're writing about the date.

The abbreviations for months are often the first three letters of the name. "January" becomes "Jan.," "November" becomes "Nov.," and so on. However, May June, and July usually don't have abbreviations since their names are short to begin with! It's the same with days of the week. The abbreviations are the first few letters. "Monday" becomes "Mon." and "Tuesday" becomes "Tues." Can you abbreviate the rest?

Figure It Out

Imagine your favorite band is playing in your town on Friday, October 24. What are the abbreviations for the day and month of the show?

Abbreviate the Date!

Monday	Tuesday	Wednesday	Thursday	Friday	Saturday	Sunday
↓	↓	↓	↓	↓	↓	↓
Mon.	**Tues.**	**Wed.**	**Thurs.**	**Fri.**	**Sat.**	**Sun.**

January → **Jan.**

February → **Feb.**

March → **Mar.**

April → **Apr.**

May → **May**

June → **June**

July → **July**

August → **Aug.**

September → **Sept.**

October → **Oct.**

November → **Nov.**

December → **Dec.**

Abbreviations for dates always begin with a capital letter and end with a period.

11

GOING PLACES

We often use abbreviations when we're writing about places, such as streets. Many street names are made of two words. The second word is usually "road," "street," "avenue," "boulevard," or "lane." These words are abbreviated as "rd.," "st.," "ave.," "blvd.," and "ln." These abbreviations usually end with a period. We save time and space by writing them this way.

We use abbreviations to write about states, too. Every state has a two-letter abbreviation. You can use these abbreviations when addressing **envelopes**, writing about where a city is located, and more.

Figure It Out

Read the following sentences. Where can you use abbreviations to make them shorter and faster? "I grew up on Elmwood Avenue in Buffalo, New York. My family moved to Houston, Texas, when I was 10 years old. We live on Oak Street now."

NAME THAT STATE!

Every state in the United States has a special abbreviation.
How many can you name?

Always capitalize both letters in state
abbreviations. They don't end with a period.

ABBREVIATIONS FOR ADDRESSES

Do you know your address? Any place that receives mail has an address. Some addresses can be long, so abbreviations are very helpful when we want to write them quickly.

Most people are familiar with the abbreviations used in addresses. If anyone picks up your letter, they'll know where it needs to go!

You already know streets and states can be abbreviated. The type of building you live in can be abbreviated, too. Apartment becomes "apt." and "building" becomes "bldg." in these cases. If a street name includes a direction, you can abbreviate it, too. You abbreviate north, south, east, and west by simply capitalizing the first letter of the word. Directions such as northeast and southwest are abbreviated with two capital letters.

Figure It Out

Use abbreviations to send a letter to the president at the White House. The address is 1600 Pennsylvania Avenue Northwest in Washington, District of Columbia. The zip code is 20500.

ABBREVIATED NAMES

Every country, **organization**, group, and club has a name. Their names are usually long because they're made of several words. That's where abbreviations come in! Abbreviations are easy ways to name something without having to spell out the entire thing. These abbreviations don't need periods.

Figure It Out

The following names can be shortened easily. Can you guess the abbreviations?

Federal Bureau of Investigation

Central Intelligence Agency

Massachusetts Institute of Technology

There's one abbreviation you should be very familiar with—USA! It's the abbreviation for the United States of America. The YMCA is another well-known abbreviation. It stands for an organization called the Young Men's Christian Association. These shortened forms are popular. They're used just as often as the full name.

We can abbreviate people's names, too. John F. Kennedy, a famous U.S. president, is often called "JFK."

USING ABBREVIATIONS TO MEASURE

Abbreviations are helpful when we measure. They make it quick and easy to record several measurements. We measure **distance** and length with inches, feet, yards, and miles. Their abbreviations are "in," "ft," "yd," and "mi." We can also measure with millimeters, centimeters, meters, and kilometers. Their abbreviations are "mm," "cm," "m," and "km." The abbreviations "mph" (miles per hour) and "km/h" (kilometers per hour) show how fast something is moving.

There are also abbreviations for weight. Small weights are measured in ounces, or "oz" for short. Large weights are measured in pounds, or "lbs" for short. Measurement abbreviations can be written with or without a period.

Figure It Out

Abbreviate the following measurements:
10 feet
65 miles per hour
83 pounds
2 centimeters

Kitchen Tools

Do you ever help out in the kitchen? If you do,
you may come across some wacky abbreviations.
Here are some of the most common!

T, tbsp	→	tablespoon
t, tsp	→	teaspoon
c	→	cup
oz	→	ounce
lb	→	pound

fl oz	→	fluid ounce
pt	→	pint
qt	→	quart
gal	→	gallon

Volume is measured in fl oz, c, pt, and gal. Can
you understand what those abbreviations mean?

EVERYDAY ABBREVIATIONS

Do you text or instant message your friends? If so, you may **recognize** some common abbreviations. "LOL" stands for "laugh out loud," "TBH" means "to be honest," and "HBU" is short for "How 'bout you?" These abbreviations are popular. However, there's a time and a place for them. You should never use these abbreviations when you're writing for school, to adults, or anything that's very important. Just use them for fun!

We live in a world of shortened words. The next time you're short on time, try using abbreviations! They help us say what we want in just a few letters.

Figure It Out

What do you think the abbreviation "abbr." stands for?

Abbreviations are a very useful part of our language.

FIGURE IT OUT ANSWERS

Page 4: We use abbreviations to save time and take up less space on a page.

Page 6: Mrs. Taylor is a married woman; Mr. Gupta is a man; Dr. Brown is a doctor; John David Sr. is the older of two people who share that name.

Page 8: You must use "a.m.," since school begins in the morning.

Page 10: Friday becomes Fri.; October becomes Oct.

Page 12: Avenue → Ave.; New York → NY; Texas → TX; Street → St.

Page 15: The President
1600 Pennsylvania Ave. NW
Washington, D.C. 20500

Page 16: FBI; CIA; MIT

Page 18: 10 ft; 65 mph; 83 lbs; 2 cm

Page 20: The abbreviation "abbr." is short for "abbreviation"!

GLOSSARY

capitalize (KAA-puh-tuh-lyz) To begin a word with a capital letter.

describe (dih-SCRYB) To tell about.

distance (DIHS-tuhns) The space between two things.

envelope (EHN-vuh-lohp) A flat paper holder for a letter.

invitation (ihn-vuh-TAY-shun) A written paper asking someone to go somewhere or do something.

organization (ohr-guh-nuh-ZAY-shun) A group of people who are together for a certain purpose.

recognize (REH-kihg-nyz) Knowing something because you've seen it before.

volume (VAHL-yoom) The amount of space something occupies.

INDEX

WEBSITES

Due to the changing nature of Internet links, PowerKids Press has developed an online list of websites related to the subject of this book. This site is updated regularly. Please use this link to access the list: www.powerkidslinks.com/cls/abbr